# MICHAEL SOUTHERN SR.

# The Illuminating Inventor

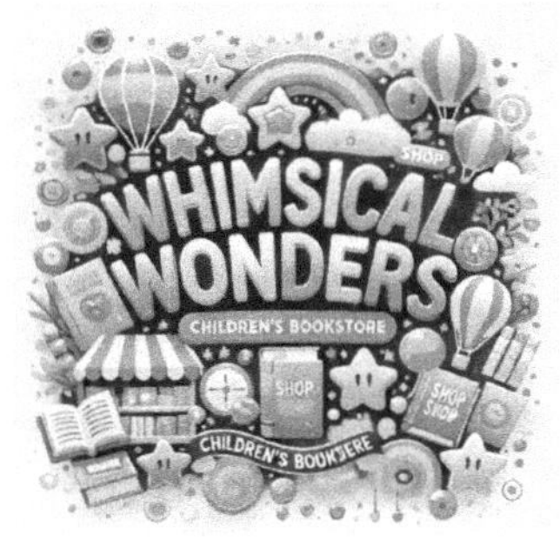

# Contents

_Prologue_

**The Spark of Genius**

Long before electric lights brightened every home, and music played from tiny devices in our pockets, there was a world filled with darkness and silence as soon as the sun set. People relied on candles and gas lamps to light their way and communicated over long distances using only their voices or written letters.

In this world of shadows and quiet, a young boy named Thomas Edison was born. From a very young age, Thomas was fascinated by the world around him. He wanted to know how things worked and dreamed of making them better. He spent his days exploring, asking questions, and experimenting with anything he could find. To him, every object held a secret, and he was determined to unlock them all.

One day, as Thomas watched the flickering flame of a candle, an idea sparked in his mind. What if he could create something even better, something that could light up the dark without the danger of fire? This small spark of an idea grew and grew, kindling a flame of curiosity and determination that would light up not just his life, but the entire world.

Little did Thomas know that his journey would take him from his small town in Ohio to becoming one of the greatest inventors the world had ever seen.

With his bright mind and endless creativity, he was about to change life as people knew it.

This is the story of how a curious boy became the man who brought light to the world. Welcome to the adventure of The Illuminating Inventor.

# Introduction

Welcome to the incredible story of Thomas Edison, a boy with big dreams and bright ideas! Thomas was just like you—curious, creative, and always asking questions. From the moment he could talk, he wanted to know how things worked and how he could make them even better.

In this book, you'll join Thomas on his journey from a small town in Ohio to becoming one of the greatest inventors of all time. You'll discover how he brought light to the world with his amazing inventions and how he never gave up, even when things got tough.

Get ready to explore the world of inventions, imagination, and endless possibilities. Remember, just like Thomas, you have the power to think big, dream bigger, and shine the brightest!

So, turn the page, and let's dive into the illuminating adventure of Thomas Edison!

# I

## Title Page

*The Illuminating Inventor by Michael Southern Sr. Illustrated by Michael Southern Sr.*

# The Curious Boy from Ohio

Once upon a time, in a small town in Ohio, there was a young boy named Thomas Edison. Thomas was not like other children; he was always asking questions and loved to explore everything around him. He would often be found taking apart his toys to see how they worked. His parents would smile and shake their heads, wondering what their curious son would get into next. Little did they know, Thomas was already dreaming up big ideas that would one day change the world. His curiosity was the spark that would light up his future.

# Young Thomas and His Big Ideas

From a young age, Thomas was always coming up with new ideas. Whether it was trying to make his own telegraph machine or inventing a new way to catch fish, his mind was always buzzing with thoughts. He spent hours in his little workshop, surrounded by tools and gadgets, tinkering with bits and pieces. His friends thought he was a bit odd, but Thomas didn't mind. He was lost in his world of inventions, where every problem was just waiting for a solution. For Thomas, every day was a new adventure, filled with endless possibilities.

# A Dream to Light Up the World

One day, while watching the sun set and darkness fill the streets, Thomas had an idea. What if there was a way to light up the night? He imagined a world where people could have light anytime they needed it, without using candles or gas lamps. This thought excited him so much that he couldn't sleep. He dreamed of creating something that could bring light into people's homes and make their lives easier. Thomas knew that if he could figure this out, it would change everything. His dream was to light up the world.

# Building the Brightest Bulb

Determined to make his dream come true, Thomas set to work. He spent hours in his workshop, trying out different materials and designs for his light bulb. He tried using paper, cotton, and even hair, but nothing seemed to work. The light bulbs would glow for a moment and then burn out. Frustrated but not discouraged, Thomas kept experimenting. He believed that with enough hard work and patience, he would find the answer. Finally, after many tries, he found that a carbon filament inside a glass bulb would keep glowing. Thomas had built the brightest bulb!

# Let There Be Light!

The day Thomas's light bulb worked was a day to remember. As he flipped the switch, the bulb lit up, filling the room with a warm, steady glow. Thomas couldn't believe his eyes. He had done it! He had invented a way to bring light into the darkness. He rushed to show his friends and family, and soon everyone was talking about the amazing new invention. The light bulb was a simple object, but it had the power to change the world. With his invention, Thomas Edison brought light to people's lives like never before.

# Edison's Invention Adventure

T homas Edison's light bulb was just the beginning. His mind was full of ideas, and he couldn't wait to bring them to life. He went on to invent the phonograph, which could record and play back sound, and the motion picture camera, which brought moving pictures to life. His workshop was always buzzing with activity, as he and his team worked on new projects. Each invention was an adventure, full of challenges and surprises. Thomas loved the thrill of discovering something new, and his inventions opened the door to a whole new world of possibilities.

# Facing Challenges and Never Giving Up

Thomas Edison didn't achieve success overnight. He faced many challenges and setbacks along the way. Many of his inventions failed, and people often doubted his ideas. But Thomas didn't let that stop him. He believed in himself and his work, and he never gave up. When his experiments didn't go as planned, he saw them as steps toward success. He famously said, "I have not failed. I've just found 10,000 ways that won't work." Thomas knew that persistence was the key to success, and he kept going no matter what obstacles came his way.

# The Power of Creativity

Through his hard work and determination, Thomas Edison showed the world the power of creativity. He believed that imagination and inventiveness could solve problems and make life better for everyone. His inventions changed the way people lived, worked, and played. The light bulb brought light to homes and streets, the phonograph brought music to life, and the motion picture camera created a whole new form of entertainment. Thomas's creativity knew no bounds, and his inventions inspired countless others to think outside the box and create new things that could change the world.

# You Can Be an Inventor Too!

As young readers, you too can be like Thomas Edison. You have the power to think outside the box and come up with new ideas. What problems do you see around you that need solving? Maybe it's a new way to organize your toys or a fun way to help your family. Don't be afraid to try new things and see what happens. Remember, every great invention started as a simple idea. You don't need a big workshop or fancy tools. All you need is your imagination and the courage to try. Who knows what amazing things you might invent?

# Dream Big, Shine Bright!

Thomas Edison's story teaches us to dream big and shine bright. He started as a curious boy with a love for tinkering and turned into one of the greatest inventors of all time. He showed us that with a little creativity and a lot of hard work, we can achieve anything we set our minds to. So, don't be afraid to dream big. Think about the things you love and how you can make them better. Use your imagination and let your ideas light up the world. Just like Thomas Edison, you can make a difference.

# Imagine a World Without Light

As you read this story, think about how Thomas Edison's inventions have impacted your life. Imagine a world without light bulbs. How would people see at night? What if there were no movies to watch or music to listen to? Thomas Edison's inventions made all these things possible. Without his creativity and hard work, the world would be a very different place. It's amazing to think about how one person's ideas can change the way we live. Edison's inventions have brought so much joy and convenience to our lives. What could you invent to change the world?

# How Edison Changed Our Lives

Thanks to Thomas Edison, we can enjoy all the wonderful things his inventions have brought us. The light bulb has brightened our homes, streets, and schools, making it possible to see clearly at any time of day. The phonograph brought music into people's homes, allowing them to listen to their favorite songs whenever they wanted. The motion picture camera created a whole new way to tell stories and share ideas. Edison's inventions have touched every part of our lives, making them easier, more enjoyable, and more connected. His legacy lives on in everything we do.

# Failure is the First Step to Success

25

R
emember, it's okay to fail and make mistakes. Thomas Edison failed over a thousand times before he successfully created the light bulb. But each failure taught him something new and brought him one step closer to success. Edison's story shows us that failure is not the end; it's just the beginning of a new opportunity. If you try something and it doesn't work, don't be discouraged. Learn from it and try again. Every great inventor, artist, and scientist has faced failure, but they didn't give up. They kept going, and so can you.

# Keep Trying, Keep Inventing

So don't be afraid to try new things and experiment with your ideas. Just like Thomas Edison, you might not get it right the first time, but that's okay. The important thing is to keep trying. Use your imagination and creativity to come up with solutions to problems you see around you. Test your ideas, and if they don't work, think about what you can do differently. Remember, every failure is a step closer to success. Who knows what amazing discoveries you may stumble upon along the way? Keep pushing forward, and never give up!

# Curiosity Leads to Amazing Discoveries

As you continue to learn and grow, remember the lessons of Thomas Edison. Be curious about the world around you. Ask questions, explore, and don't be afraid to take things apart to see how they work. Curiosity is the key to discovery, and it's what drives inventors like Edison to create new things. When you're curious, you open the door to endless possibilities. You might find a new way to do something, solve a problem, or even invent something completely new. So stay curious, keep learning, and let your imagination lead the way.

# Your Ideas Can Change the World

The world is full of endless possibilities just waiting for you to explore. You have the power to change the world with your ideas, just like Thomas Edison did. Whether it's a new invention, a creative solution to a problem, or a way to make people's lives better, your ideas matter. Don't be afraid to share them and bring them to life. Remember, every great invention started as a simple idea. The light bulb, the phonograph, the motion picture camera—they all began with a thought. Your ideas can make a difference, so dream big and shine bright.

# A Boy with a Bright Future

Thomas Edison was once a young boy with a curious mind and a love for tinkering. He didn't know it then, but his big ideas would one day change the world. He showed us that anyone, no matter how small, can make a big impact. All it takes is curiosity, creativity, and a lot of hard work. Edison's story is a reminder that the future is full of possibilities. So, as you grow up and explore the world, remember that you too have the power to make a difference. Your future is bright, just like Edison's.

# The Amazing Life of Thomas Edison

As you reflect on the life of Thomas Edison, think about all the incredible things he achieved. From his early days as a curious boy in Ohio to his groundbreaking inventions that changed the world, Edison's story is one of creativity, perseverance, and inspiration. He showed us that anything is possible if we believe in ourselves and work hard. His inventions have brought light, sound, and motion into our lives, making the world a brighter and more exciting place. Edison's amazing life reminds us that we all have the power to make a difference.

# Be Bold, Be Creative, Be You

As you go out into the world, remember to be like Thomas Edison. Be bold in your ideas, creative in your thinking, and true to yourself. Don't be afraid to stand out and try new things. The world needs people who think differently, who are willing to take risks and explore new possibilities. Edison's inventions changed the world because he wasn't afraid to dream big and follow his passion. You can do the same. Be brave, be inventive, and let your light shine. The future is yours to shape, so go out there and make it a bright one.

# Shine Like Edison: The End

And with that, we come to the end of our story. We hope you have enjoyed learning about the illuminating inventor, Thomas Edison, and his incredible journey of discovery and innovation. Remember, the power to change the world lies within you. Just like Edison, you have the ability to dream big, think creatively, and never give up. Let your light shine bright, and be the inventor of your own destiny. Who knows what incredible things you may achieve? The world is waiting for your ideas, so go out there and make it a bright one!

# About the Author

Michael Southern Sr. is a dedicated writer and storyteller who delights in bringing the wonders of the world to young minds. Through his site, WhimsicalWonders, he creates enchanting and educational books for children, aiming to inspire curiosity and a love for learning. Michael believes that every story has the power to ignite imagination and spark joy, especially in the hearts of young readers.

Drawing from his diverse background as a combat veteran and years in law enforcement, Michael brings a unique perspective to his stories, combining adventure with valuable life lessons. His passion for teaching and his creative storytelling make his books a favorite among children and parents alike.

Michael lives with his wife, who runs her own homemade jam business, Nana's Kitchen Kreations, and their three children. In his free time, he enjoys exploring nature, spending quality time with his family, and dreaming up new stories to captivate and educate young readers.

In David and the Giant: The Boy Who Defeated Goliath, young readers are taken on a thrilling journey through the ancient lands of Israel. This captivating story brings to life the classic tale of a brave shepherd boy named David, who, armed with only a slingshot and his unwavering faith, stands up to the mighty giant Goliath. Despite the odds, David's courage and belief in himself prove that even the smallest person can make a big difference. Filled with adventure, lessons in bravery, and the power of believing in oneself, this book is perfect for inspiring children to overcome their fears and challenges.

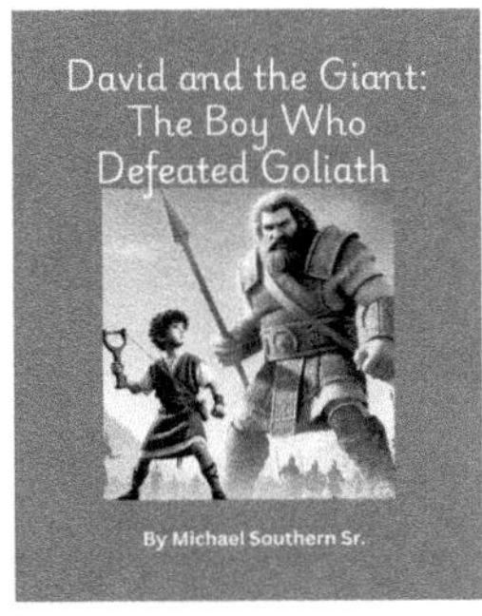

**David and the Giant: The Boy Who Defeated Goliath**

https://www.etsy.com/listing/1787291813/david-and-the-giant-the-boy-who-defeated?ref=listings_manager_grid

Step into the ancient world of Israel and meet David, a young shepherd boy with a heart full of courage. When a fearsome giant named Goliath threatens his people, everyone is too scared to fight—everyone except David. Armed with only a slingshot and his unshakeable faith, David faces the giant in a battle that will be remembered for generations.

*David and the Giant: The Boy Who Defeated Goliath* is an inspiring tale of bravery, faith, and the power of believing in oneself. Perfect for young readers, this story shows that even the smallest among us can do great things. Join David on his heroic adventure and discover the true meaning of courage!